City in a garden: parks and plans

and Parks

Judith Paine McBrien
Illustrated by Debra McQueen
Maps by Malcolm Edgerton

Edited by Samantha Lee Kelly

Published by Perspectives*Press*
Wilmette

Copyright ©1996 Perspectives International Inc.
Printed in the United States of America

All rights reserved. No part of this publication may be reproduced
or transmitted in any form or by any means, electronic or mechanical,
including photocopy, recording, or any information storage and
retrieval system, without permission in writing from the publisher,
Perspectives*Press*, Box 565, Wilmette, IL 60091.

Book Design by Victoria Behm
Library of Congress Catalogue Card Number: 93-092707
ISBN 1-880005-06-9

To the Department of Research and Planning, Chicago Park District

for promoting a greater understanding of Chicago's parks.

Introduction

Since our earliest beginnings, we Chicagoans have worked tirelessly to transform our city's motto into truth. "Urbs in Horto," we have said of this city of work and commerce, of grit and hustle: City in a Garden.

Uttered at first perhaps as a kind of wishful thinking to the swamps and barren wildness of the natural landscape, Chicago boosters dreamt of a civilized and idyllic image for a rough frontier outpost.

They also made good on their promise. Within little more than thirty years after becoming a city in 1837, Chicago had planned a vast park and boulevard system that set the standard for park development in America.

As great industry thrived, as the tumult of steel mill and stockyard roared, park plans were gradually implemented. The great parks, Jackson, Washington, Douglas, Garfield, Grant, Lincoln, Humboldt, and many later smaller parks were tied together by a green encircling ribbon of boulevards that stretched open space throughout Chicago's neighborhoods. The cooling shore of Lake Michigan too became our playground, with nearly thirty miles of public parkland with beaches, harbors, and recreational facilities.

As Chicago became a true city citizen of the world, we created more plans for the future that would secure Chicago's place as a most distinguished and beautiful metropolis. The core of this greatness: our parks, our civic sense, our public realm.

Join us in this fourth of five parts in the story of making Chicago as we discover a City in a Garden.

Howard S. Decker, AIA
Landmarks Preservation Council of Illinois

1 Boulevard System

Drexel and South Open Parkway (now Martin Luther King Drive)
The Midway; Garfield, Western, 31st, California, 24th, Marshall,
Independence, Central Park, Franklin, Sacramento, Humboldt,
Kedzie, Logan, Diversey Parkway, Lake Shore Drive
Planned 1869; implemented in sections

When civic leaders incorporated Chicago as a city in 1837, they looked at the flat, swampy, windswept site and called it *Urbs in Horto*, "City in a Garden." To make a reality of this vision, legislation creating Chicago's comprehensive park system was approved in 1869-70, and the boulevards were an integral part of the plan. These wide, straight roadways, bordered or centered with grassy medians and formal tree allees, were planned to connect projected parks south, west, and north of the Chicago River forming a "greenway" completely encircling the fast-growing city. Each of the three independent park districts had its own designers, responsible for both parks and boulevards. The South Parks District hired Frederick Law Olmsted (1822-1903) and Calvert Vaux (1824-1895); William Le Baron Jenney (1832-1907) was selected by the West Parks District. On the north side, development occurred before land adequate for the typical 250-foot boulevard width was secured by the Lincoln Park District, so Diversey Parkway was not fully implemented and is only 66 feet wide. Intended to provide orderly circulation through the city as well as corridors of light and space, these boulevards remain some of Chicago's principal roadways as well as being a remarkable urban amenity.

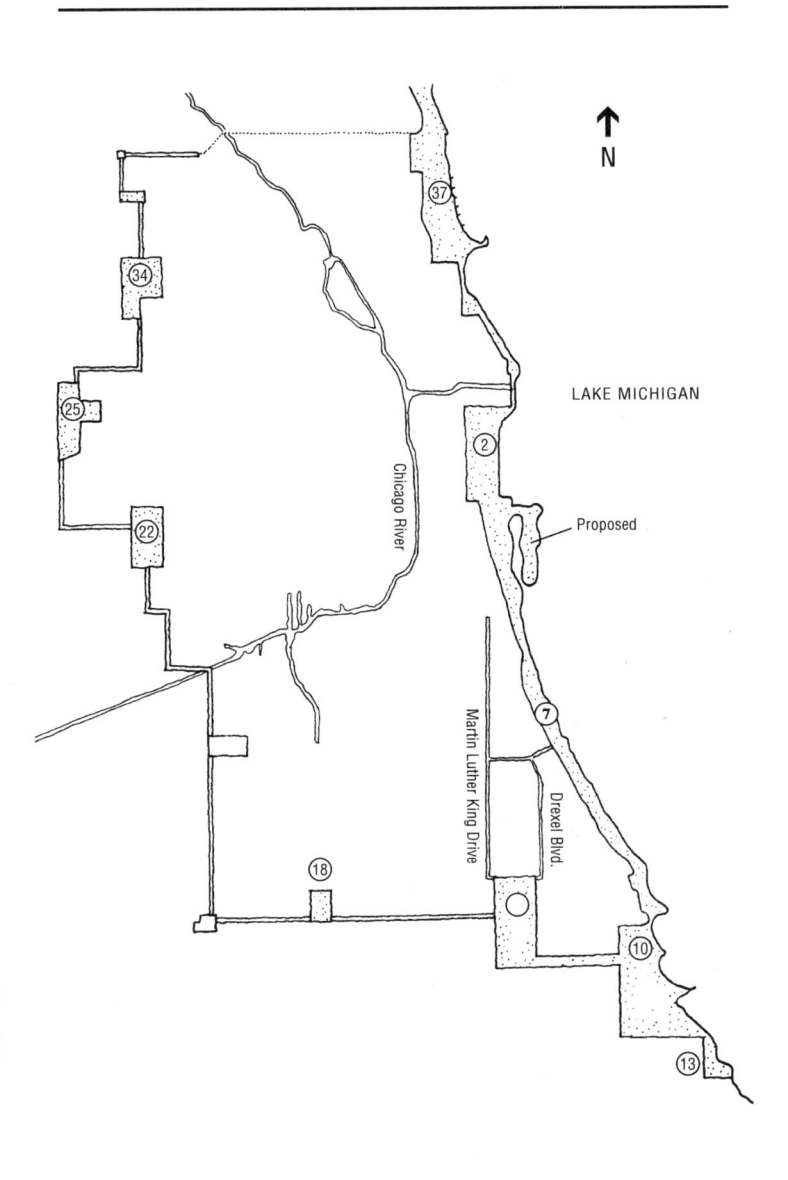

Boulevard and Park System 1

2 Grant Park

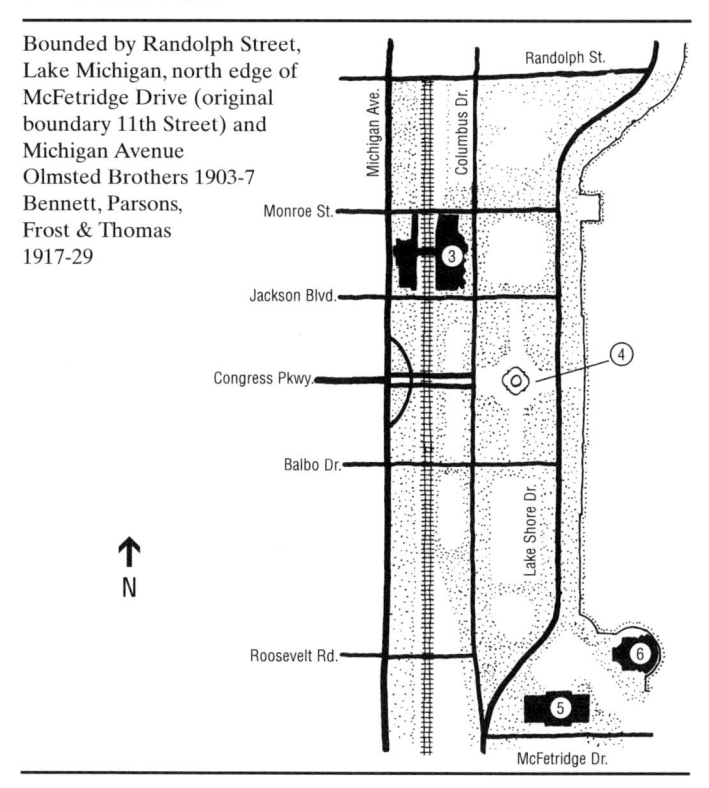

Bounded by Randolph Street,
Lake Michigan, north edge of
McFetridge Drive (original
boundary 11th Street) and
Michigan Avenue
Olmsted Brothers 1903-7
Bennett, Parsons,
Frost & Thomas
1917-29

Grant Park is among Chicago's oldest parks and has perhaps the most dramatic story. It began as Lake Park, a slender sliver of land between Lake Michigan and Michigan Avenue designated "forever open, clear and free" in 1836. Later, debris from the Great Fire of 1871 was pushed into the lake, expanding the park eastward to the Illinois Central railroad tracks, but with no particular landscape plan. As Chicago became more self-conscious in the 1890s, numerous schemes were proposed to enlarge the park creating a grand civic lawn to showcase the city and its greatest natural amenity, Lake Michigan. Most ideas included plans for large buildings in the park. But one influential citizen, A. Montgomery Ward, believed that the lakefront should remain true to its original intention as open space for all people. Despite great criticism, he brought lawsuits for twenty years until he won his case in 1911. After World War I, a formal plan based on French prototypes was implemented by the firm Bennett, Parsons, Frost & Thomas. Notice how, like an architect's blueprint, "rooms" are created of lawn sections, formal flower beds and rows of trees and how architectural elements such as balustrades and pylons are used to enliven the overall Beaux Arts design.

Art Institute of Chicago 3

Michigan Avenue at Adams Street
Shepley, Rutan and Coolidge
1892-93
Additions: McKinlock Court, Coolidge and Hodgdon 1924; Ferguson Building, Holabird and Root 1958; Morton Wings, Shaw, Metz and Associates 1962; Rubloff Building, Skidmore, Owings & Merrill 1976; Reconstruction of the Stock Exchange Trading Room, Vinci/Kenny 1977; Rice Building, Hammond, Beeby, and Babka 1988

Built in conjunction with the World's Columbian Exposition of 1893, the limestone Art Institute of Chicago was designed in the Beaux Arts style so prevalent at the fair. Its symmetrical massing and classical decorative elements create a dignified exterior. The first story walls are of rusticated limestone; the second, taller story has a smooth ashlar finish punctuated by a series of sculpture arcades and capped by a frieze reproducing the Parthenon's Panathenaic procession. Note the artists' names inscribed on the architrave. Interior spaces are organized in corridors off a grand central staircase. Established in 1879 as the Academy of Fine Arts, the museum grew quickly; by 1893 it had replaced W. W. Boyington's 1873 Inter-State Exposition building in Lake (now Grant) Park. Sculptor Edward Kemeys (1843-1907) is responsible for the famous lions, which have flanked the entrances since 1894. Over the past century, many additions have been constructed; the museum and the School of the Art Institute now straddle the Metra tracks that once bound the museum's east facade. Gardens on the south, designed by landscape architect Dan Kiley, and on the north, by Hanna/Olin, are important components of the museum's distinguished design tradition.

4 Clarence Buckingham Fountain

East End of Congress Drive at Columbus Drive
Marcel Francois Loyau & Jacques Lambert
Bennett, Parsons & Frost, Architects
1927
Renovation: Harry Weese & Associates 1995

Buckingham Fountain is Grant Park's focal point, and like the park, is modeled on French prototypes. It was commissioned in 1927 by Kate Buckingham to honor her late brother Clarence, a trustee of the Art Institute, but also to bring European monumentality to Chicago. Dramatically situated at the eastern terminus of Congress Parkway and along a north-south axis of formal rose gardens and stately elms, the fountain lies in a scalloped-edge pool 280 feet across, surrounded by four pairs of bronze sea creatures spouting water. Its three tiers of pink marble basins, rising 25 feet above ground level, are supported on the lower levels by brackets ornamented with carved seaweed and jet-equipped saucers; the topmost basin rests on a central pedestal ringed by eight square columns. The design, an Art Deco re-interpretation of Versailles' Bassin de Latone, won French sculptor M.F. Loyau the Prix National at the 1927 Paris Salon. Its symbolism, however, is wholly native: the base pool represents Lake Michigan, while its bronze inhabitants symbolize the bordering states. The water-jets and color spotlights, originally choreographed by hand from an underground control room, were computerized by Harry Weese & Associates as part of a major 1995 renovation.

Field Museum of Natural History 5

Roosevelt Road at Lake Shore Drive
D. H. Burnham & Co. 1909-1912
Graham, Burnham & Co. 1912-17
Graham, Anderson, Probst and White 1917-1920
Renovation: Harry Weese & Associates 1977

At 775,000 square feet of floor area, the Field Museum is one of the largest museum buildings in the world. The collection originated with the World's Columbian Exposition in 1893, but only in 1906, when Marshall Field donated $8 million to the museum, could a permanent home be established. Architect Daniel Burnham (1846-1912) situated the museum in Grant Park as the eastern focal point of Congress Parkway as can be seen in the 1909 Plan of Chicago, but A. Montgomery Ward's suits to keep Grant Park free of buildings delayed construction. The bitter conflict was settled when Stanley Field persuaded the Illinois Central to donate two acres of lakefront landfill just south of Roosevelt Road for the new museum. A symmetrical plan centers on the main pavilion, where entrances on north and south facades access a large central hall; exhibition spaces flank this hall, and continue in smaller, adjacent pavilions. The equally symmetrical facade is modeled on the Erechtheion, a 5th-century B.C. Greek temple. Fountains in the central hall, as well as glass partitions behind the giant entrance columns, were added by Harry Weese & Associates in 1977.

6 John G. Shedd Aquarium

1200 South Lake Shore Drive
Graham, Anderson, Probst and White
1929
Oceanarium addition: Lohan Associates 1991

A year before his death in 1926, John G. Shedd, former president and chairman of the board of Marshall Field Co., agreed to provide $3 million for the construction of an aquarium adjacent to the new Field Museum of Natural History. When it opened in 1930, it was the first in the United States to maintain a collection of both fresh-water and salt-water aquatic life. The firm of Graham, Anderson, Probst & White, which had also designed the Field Museum (see # 5) and such Chicago landmarks as the Wrigley Building and the Merchandise Mart, received the commission. Chief designer Peirce Anderson (1870-1936) used his Beaux Arts training to create a modified classical temple: a Greek cross with the corners partially filled in to create an octagon. An octagonal tower, roofed with a translucent skylight, rises above the central rotunda, around which lie a series of exhibit halls. The entrance portico on the west facade is based on a Greek Doric temple. The exterior, clad with white Georgia marble, mirrors the nearby Field Museum. The Oceanarium, designed by Lohan Associates in 1991, wraps around the rear of the building; its modern, steel-and-glass exterior contrasts strikingly with the original structure.

Burnham Park 7

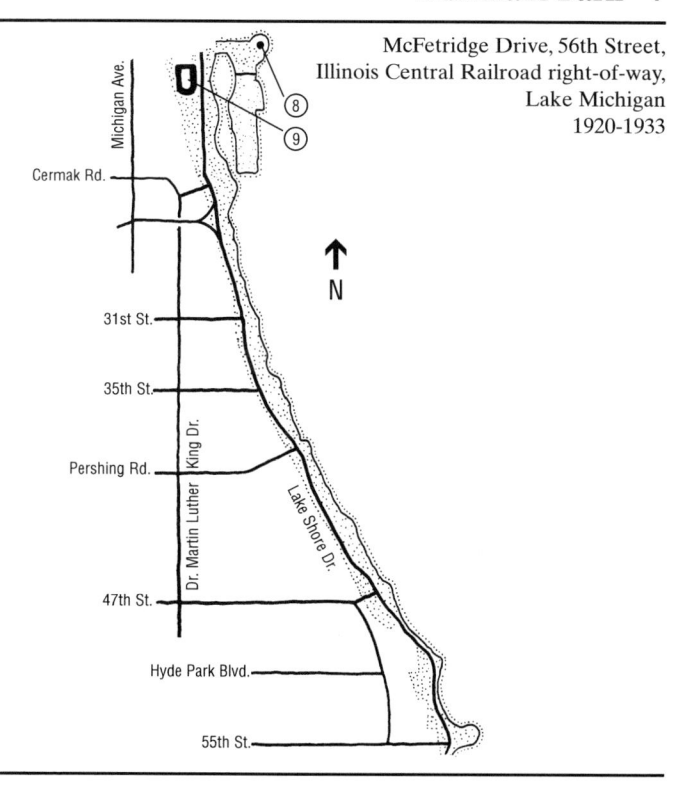

McFetridge Drive, 56th Street,
Illinois Central Railroad right-of-way,
Lake Michigan
1920-1933

The 1909 Plan of Chicago proposed a series of man-made islands off Chicago's lakefront coast, but only Northerly Island, which connects to the northern end of Burnham Park via Solidarity Drive, was built. Because the park and island were completely new, they were not immediately subject to the "forever open, clear and free" stipulation attached to Grant Park, so various cultural institutions located there (see # 8 and # 9). When landfill was completed, Northerly Island Park was used as the site for the 1933-34 World's Fair, "A Century of Progress." After World War II, the Meigs Field Airport occupied the southern island section, but when the airport lease expired in 1996, plans began, with a design team led by architect John MacManus (b. 1954), to return the site to its original open space purpose. The rerouting of Lake Shore Drive, which once split into north/south lanes at the Field Museum, to the west side of this institution creates a cultural campus at the park's north end. Promontory Point is the highlight of the park's southern end at 55th St. Designed in 1937 by Alfred Caldwell, a disciple of landscape architect Jens Jensen (1860-1951), it offers a distinctive regional landscape, including native plantings such as hawthorn trees as well as a council ring.

8 Adler Planetarium & Astronomical Museum

Ernest A. Grunsfeld, Jr.
1300 South Lake Shore Drive
1930
Entrance addition: Lohan Associates 1981

German emigré Max Adler commissioned this planetarium, among the first in the western hemisphere, in the hope that observation of the heavens would instill a desire for peace by illustrating that "all mankind rich and poor, powerful and weak, as well as all nations here and abroad constitute part of one universe." The building's serenely geometric, twelve-sided form, clad in smoothly finished granite and capped by a copper dome, suggests a classical temple but with an historical visual vocabulary suited to the scientific novelty of its function; it earned architect Ernest A. Grunsfeld, Jr. (1897-1970), a Gold Medal from the American Institute of Architects in 1930. A series of setbacks creates terraces that were used for astronomical observation before city lights reduced visibility. Vertical fluting highlights the building's twelve corners, as do sculptor Alfonso Ianelli's (1888-1965) bronze plaques, which depict the twelve zodiacal constellations according to the descriptions of the 2nd-century Greek astronomer Ptolemy. Bronze-covered entrance doors originally led to the auditorium, situated under the dome, while encircling rooms contain the Adler's collection of astronomical instruments. Due to additions of 1973 and 1981, access is now through a steel-and-glass pavilion that leads to a lower-level exhibition and theater space.

Soldier Field 9

16th Street and Lake Shore Drive
Holabird & Roche
1922-1926

A Grant Park stadium was included in the 1909 Plan of Chicago, but only in 1919, after landfill had created additional park space, was an architectural competition held for its design. Holabird & Roche, a firm responsible for many important Chicago School skyscrapers, won with an unusual U-shaped design that offered versatility, classical grandeur, and visual integration in a larger urban complex. Long (1375 ft.) and narrow (375 ft.), it could house smaller events by clustering spectators in the rounded, southern end, or accommodate large crowds along its whole length. Doors and windows in the perimeter wall are outlined with simple classical moldings, while above the east and west flanks, grandly scaled Doric colonnades — double rows of fluted columns supporting simple entablatures — terminate in Doric temples. Its open, northern end originally offered views of the Field Museum, linking the stadium with surrounding structures. However, since 1939 the Chicago Park District headquarters has blocked views to the north, while press- and skyboxes added in 1981 obstruct interior views of the colonnades. Renamed Soldier Field in 1925 to honor World War I soldiers, it is now the home of the Chicago Bears football team.

10   Jackson Park

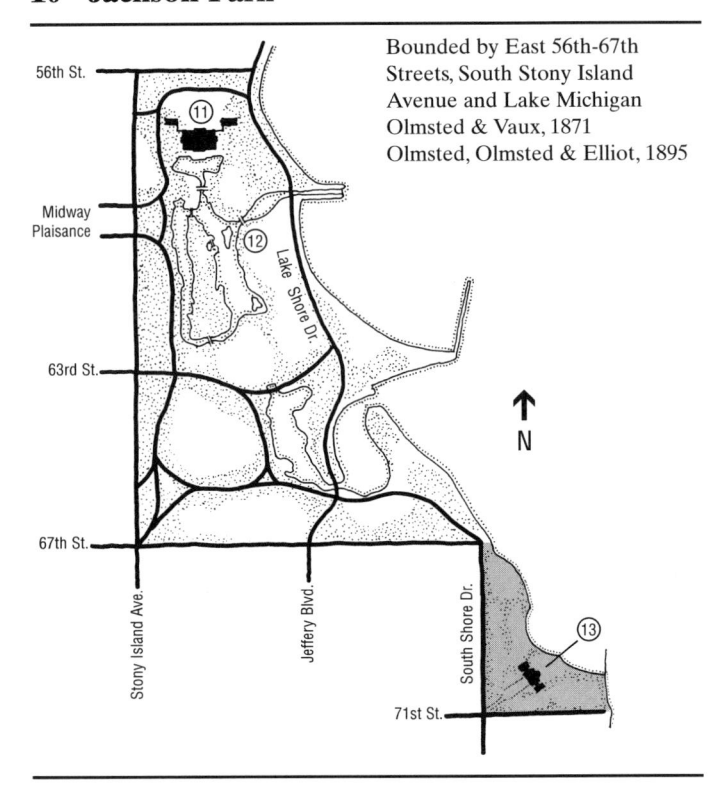

Bounded by East 56th-67th
Streets, South Stony Island
Avenue and Lake Michigan
Olmsted & Vaux, 1871
Olmsted, Olmsted & Elliot, 1895

South Park, comprising present-day Jackson Park on the lakefront, Washington Park (see # 14) to the west, and the connecting Midway Plaisance, was designed by Olmsted and Vaux in 1871. Like their earlier great design, New York's Central Park, it represents a pastoral conception of the park as a refuge from urban stress. The primary theme is aquatic: a channel cut through the beachfront at 59th St. connected a series of lagoons, meant to lead via canals in the Midway Plaisance to a small lake in Washington Park. Though the northern end of the "Lower Division," or Jackson Park saw some development, work began in earnest when the park was chosen as the site of the 1893 World's Columbian Exposition. Although the Midway canals were never dug, a huge formal basin, the Court of Honor was constructed as well as a large lagoon and island. The historic Lagoon as well as the Wooded Island survive largely as created for the fair, as does the Museum of Science and Industry (see # 11) and the Columbia Basin at the park's northern border. After the fair, Jackson Park was redesigned by Olmsted, his son and partner, John Charles Olmsted (1852-1920) and Charles Elliot (1859-97).

Museum of Science and Industry   11

South Lake Shore Drive at East 57th Street
D.H. Burnham & Co.
1893
Reconstruction: Graham, Anderson,
Probst and White 1929-1940

This structure, originally the Fine Arts Building of the 1893 World's Columbian Exposition, is an outstanding example of Beaux Arts architecture. Charles Atwood (1840-95), chief designer at D.H. Burnham & Co., first planned a rectangular pavilion capped by a low, Pantheonesque dome, with centrally placed entrances on each facade providing access to interior cross-halls. These entrances, with Ionic columns supporting triangular pediments, were modeled on the Erechtheion (see # 5); similarly, a series of porches echo the Erechtheion's Porch of Caryatids, with columns in the shape of walking female figures exactly reproduced from the original. When submissions to the Fine Arts exhibit exceeded expectations, Atwood added two subsidiary pavilions which retain the structure's symmetry and continue its Ionic motif. Originally intended to be temporary, the building survived the Exposition's end by housing the Field Museum of Natural History until 1920. It escaped a second threat of destruction in 1927 when Julius Rosenwald, chairman of Sears, Roebuck & Co., offered $3 million to establish it as a science museum. Atwood's original exterior forms and details were reproduced in more permanent Bedford limestone, while interior spaces, notably a new Art Deco rotunda, were redesigned. The Henry Crown Space Center was added in 1986.

12 Japanese Pavilion and Garden

Wooded Island, East side
Reconstruction and additions: Chicago Park District
1984, 1991

The Ho-o-den Palace, a group of three Japanese pavilions constructed on the Wooded Island for the 1893 World's Columbian Exposition, is believed to have strongly influenced Frank Lloyd Wright in the early development of his Prairie style architecture. It was preserved until World War II, when anti-Japanese sentiment led to the razing of the structures and abandonment of the gardens. In 1981, the Design Division of the Chicago Park District designed a new garden on the site, including a tea house, waterfall, stone lanterns, and an arched "moon bridge." It was renamed the Osaka Garden in 1994, when the City of Osaka (Japan) donated a new formal entrance gate, fence, and other landscape improvements designed by landscape architect Koichi Kobayashi. The entrance gate, following traditional Japanese principles, highlights beautifully executed wood joinery, as does the open-air tea house with its flared roof and wood-edged floor. Looking north from the tea-house, the moon bridge is visible, connecting the main gardens to a tiny island hosting a traditional Japanese landscape. Stone lanterns ornamented with flared tops and Japanese carving are scattered throughout the garden; from the bridge is a view of the Museum of Science and Industry (see # 11) to the north.

South Shore Cultural Center 13

7059 South South Shore Drive
Marshall and Fox
1916
Renovation: Norman De Haan Associates 1983

Formerly South Shore Country Club

The South Shore Country Club, occupying a magnificent 65-acre site on Lake Michigan, was founded in 1906 as a "country club in town" for the professional South Shore community. The present clubhouse replaced the original in 1916, when increased membership necessitated larger facilities; both were designed by Marshall and Fox, a team responsible for numerous upscale Chicago hotels, including the Drake and the Blackstone. A vaguely Mediterranean feel is provided by the simple, painted stucco exterior and clay-tiled roof. The T-shaped plan is well-suited to entertainment on a grand scale. The five-story central section originally contained offices, guest rooms for club members, and public rooms for card playing, billiards, and a library; a two-story-high promenade connects it to single-story pavilions on the north, south, and east. These pavilions, which house a solarium, ballroom, and dining room, open onto the park grounds through French doors. The club prospered until the 1960s, when membership declined and the club disbanded in 1974. The Chicago Park District then acquired the grounds and buildings, now used as a cultural center and public park.

14 Washington Park

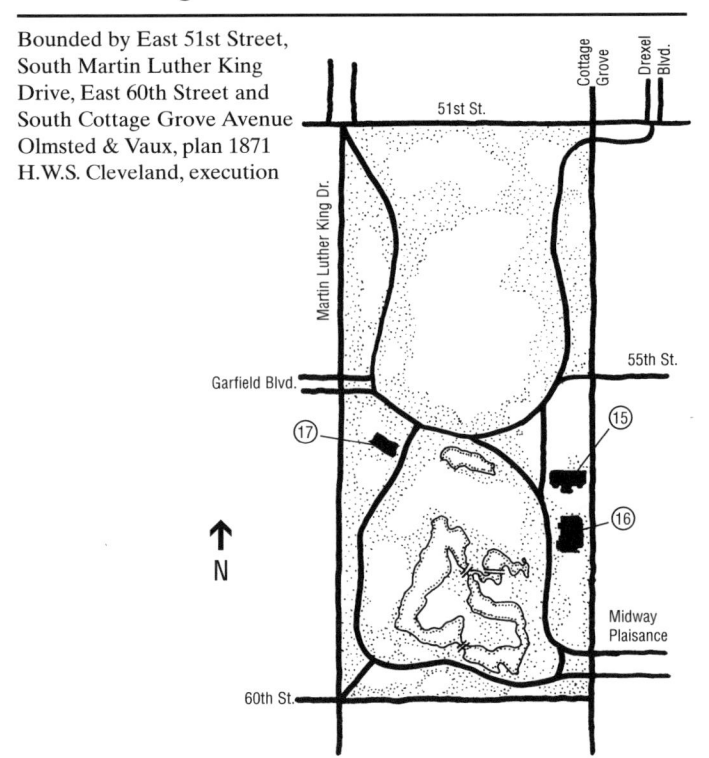

Bounded by East 51st Street,
South Martin Luther King
Drive, East 60th Street and
South Cottage Grove Avenue
Olmsted & Vaux, plan 1871
H.W.S. Cleveland, execution

Planned as the "Upper Division" of a larger South Park complex, Washington Park adapts the pastoral theme of landscape architects Olmsted & Vaux to an inland setting. The aquatic theme so prevalent in the "Lower Division," Jackson Park (see # 10), is represented here only in the southern half of the park, where a pond and an islanded lagoon, originally meant to connect via canals in the Midway to the lakefront, are surrounded by extensive tree plantings. This southern half contrasts with the northern zone, where a 100-acre meadow highlights the natural prairie terrain. This huge open ground provided space for parades and special events, where the whole community could assemble, but more often sheep grazed there. Olmsted intended to create places of calm and ease, where natural settings refreshed the human spirit. Buildings are few and confined to the park's perimeter. H.W.S. Cleveland (1814-1900), a talented landscape designer in his own right, implemented Olmsted & Vaux's plan. Washington Park is also the terminus of three boulevards (see # 1) Garfield to the west; Drexel and South Open Parkway (now Martin Luther King Drive) to the north.

Du Sable Museum of African-American History 15

740 East 56th Place
D.H. Burnham & Co.
1910
Addition: Wendell Campbell Associates 1992

Formerly the South Park Commission Administration Building

Like the Refectory to the west (see # 17), this building was designed by D. H. Burnham & Co., but while the Refectory embodies the simplicity of outdoor pleasures, this structure exudes a formal classicism. It is symmetrical in plan and elevation in the Beaux Arts tradition and faces north toward an area originally conceived as formal gardens. On this main, northern facade, a central entrance pavilion projects slightly from flanking wings and rises to a gabled roof reminiscent of a triangular pediment. The entrance itself, flanked by paired concrete pilasters with terra cotta capitals, is defined by doors and by a multi-paned transom set within a tall, flattened-arch opening; above, classical swags drape from a concrete shield. Though Classical Revival in style, the building is made of the same sturdy, aggregate concrete, known as marblecrete, used by the firm for other park buildings. A new wing designed by Wendell Campbell Associates in 1992 added gallery space and a theater; its exterior, of lightly sanded pre-cast concrete, meshes well with the original structure. Originally built as the headquarters for the South Parks Commission, the building now houses the Du Sable Museum of African-American History.

16 Washington Park Drama and Rigger Shop

Payne Drive south of 57th Street
Burnham & Root
1880

This unusual roundhouse, which now houses the scenery shops for Chicago Park District theaters, was originally built as a stable in 1880 and is the oldest surviving structure in Washington Park. Walls are built of rock-faced Joliet limestone laid in a random ashlar pattern, and are topped by a ring of clerestory windows and a cupola executed in sheet metal. It is one of the earliest buildings by the leading Chicago firm Burnham & Root. D. H. Burnham had tried several careers, including politics, before an apprenticeship with William LeBaron Jenney led him to choose architecture as his life's work. John Wellborn Root (1850-1891), Georgia-born and educated in civil engineering at New York University, came to Chicago after the 1871 fire. The two men met in 1872 while working for the firm Carter, Drake and Wight; the next year, while still in their twenties, they formed their own architectural practice. Their other Chicago commissions include the Rookery Building (1888) and the first phase of the Monadnock Building (1891). After Root's death Burnham formed an influential solo practice; his 1909 Plan of Chicago was crucial in the city's development, but as this early commission shows, he was already involved in the development of Chicago's public spaces at the start of his career.

Washington Park Refectory 17

Pool and Russell Drives
D.H. Burnham & Co.
1891
Renovation: A. Epstein & Sons with Dubin, Dubin & Moutoussamy and Hasbrouck Peterson Associates 1992

Also known as the Pool and Locker Building

The Washington Park Refectory was built in 1891 near the site originally designated by landscape designer Frederick Law Olmsted: in the southern portion of the park but overlooking the Parade Ground open meadow to the north. As designed by D. H. Burnham & Co., it conveys a sense of simplicity and airy openness. A two-story central section, rectangular in plan, is flanked by single-story wings; all are built of buff Roman brick and trimmed in white glazed terra cotta. A continuous arcade surrounds the building on three sides, supported by simple unfluted terra cotta columns; a similar arcade, of Ionic terra cotta columns, adorns the second story, while four open-air towers grace the hipped roof above. The sense of spaciousness originally continued in the interior where large refreshment rooms were housed on each floor of the central section. The Refectory, like the park, was intended to encourage development in the adjacent community of Hyde Park by providing attractive public pleasure grounds. Additions and alterations done in 1936 were consistent with this intention: a pool stadium was built just to the south, and interior alterations in the Refectory transformed it into a pool locker facility.

18 Sherman Park

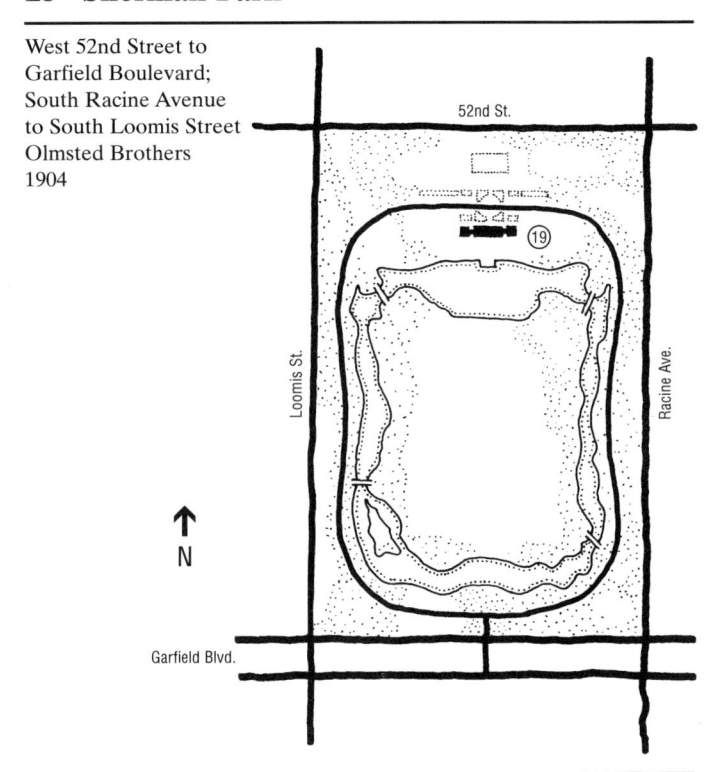

West 52nd Street to
Garfield Boulevard;
South Racine Avenue
to South Loomis Street
Olmsted Brothers
1904

Built in 1904, 60-acre Sherman Park was one of Chicago's first and most beautiful neighborhood parks. It was named for John B. Sherman, who was head of the nearby Union Stock Yards, and also Daniel H. Burnham's father-in-law. The Olmsted Brothers, John Charles and Frederick Law Olmsted, Jr. (1870-1957) were sons of Frederick Law Olmsted and successors to their father's landscape architecture practice. They continued to draw on the older conception of the park as bucolic retreat while incorporating new demands. The southern two-thirds of the park was transformed from flat, swampy terrain into a rolling topography of bermed perimeters and informal, naturalistic plantings. A lagoon surrounding a large, meadow-covered island dominates the pastoral landscape. Moving north, however, the design becomes formal: wandering paths straighten into a circular concourse lined by evenly spaced trees, while hilly berms give way to a continuous elevated earthen platform. Here are clustered all the park's facilities, which represent the newer park philosophy of structured recreation for the city's growing population of working poor. Complementing their formal setting with classical motifs, these buildings also overlook the southern lagoon from their raised platform; the overall effect is one of varied but integrated design.

Sherman Park Fieldhouse 19

Sherman Park
D.H. Burnham & Co.
1904-5

The Sherman Park Fieldhouse was designed by architects D. H. Burnham & Co., who collaborated with the Olmsted Brothers on this and other neighborhood parks in the South Parks District. The primary objective was to provide a variety of disciplined, constructive leisure activities to the area's immigrant population. The fieldhouse is the hub of the resulting recreational complex: its two-story central building housed an auditorium, while flanking single-story octagonal pavilions served as club rooms. Men's and women's gymnasia were placed to the north and linked visually to the main structure through repeated use of pergolas. Other facilities, such as a children's playground and a wading pool, were also incorporated in the complex. In addition to function, however, D. H. Burnham & Co. wished the design to be visually uplifting. The inexpensive aggregate concrete, or marblecrete, used for construction was adorned with integrally cast classical ornament; identical north and south facades are pierced by Palladian windows separated by classical pilasters. A diamond-patterned band runs beneath the eaves of the fieldhouse's hipped roof and is repeated in surrounding structures. The resulting design was both useful and beautiful, complementing the landscape plan in which it is set.

20 Fuller Park

45th to 46th Place, South Princeton Avenue to South Stewart Avenue
Olmsted Brothers
1905

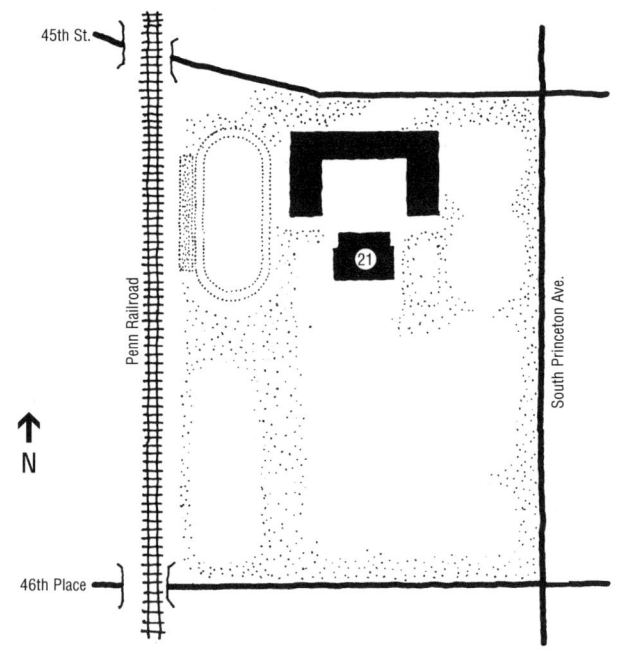

By 1901, 75% of Chicago's urban population was comprised of immigrant industrial laborers and their children. Housed in squalid tenements with few amenities, isolated from older, more prosperous neighborhoods and from the city's grand pleasure grounds, they exemplified the social ills resulting from a booming industrial economy. In response, a citywide progressive movement was launched to improve living conditions and integrate these immigrant enclaves into the social fabric. In addition to Jane Addams' Hull House, the movement included the South Parks Commission's newly-conceived neighborhood parks. In these new parks, gymnasia, playing fields, and often branches of the public library were included, as well as fieldhouses with instructive murals depicting great moments in American history. Fuller Park, built in 1905, is a typical example of these parks. Located just east of the then-booming Union Stockyards, it served one of Chicago's most neglected communities, and like most such parks was severely limited in size. The compact and ingenious design developed by the Olmsted Brothers and D. H. Burnham & Co. illustrates the creativity devoted to these small park projects.

Fuller Park Fieldhouse 21

Fuller Park
D.H. Burnham & Co.
1910

Fuller Park is a classic example of the challenges facing Chicago's innovative neighborhood parks and their successful resolution. On a small plot bordered by cramped tenements and railroad tracks, it offered both open "breathing space" and the requisite organized recreation facilities housed in a new building type, the Park Fieldhouse. With the southern portion reserved for playing fields, D. H. Burnham & Co. clustered the buildings at the north end. Gymnasia and locker rooms occupy a flattened "U"-shaped building, opening to the south. The fieldhouse proper sits in this opening, effectively closing the courtyard and connecting to the gymnasia via loggias. Its main facade, overlooking the playing fields to the south, features three round-arch windows set within peaked dormers; the east and west elevations echo this facade, with rounded Palladian windows and peaked roof gables. The entire complex is made of an economical "marblecrete" often used in parks buildings, but with much cast-in-place classical ornament, such as fluted pilasters and keystones; a waffled diamond pattern ornaments upper wall areas. A children's spray pool lies to the east, and a small poolhouse to the southwest. Most ingenious is the outdoor track to the west, which utilized the existing railroad embankment to support stadium seating.

22 Douglas Park

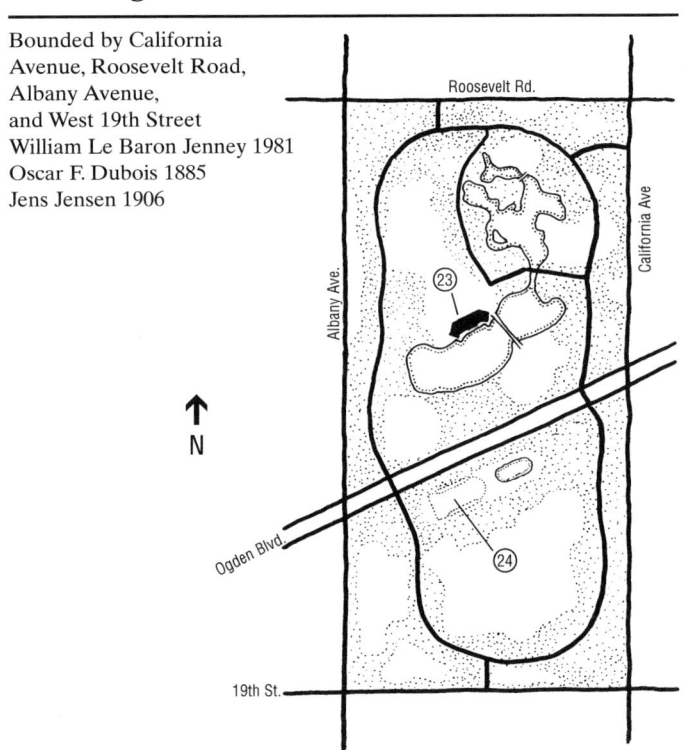

Bounded by California
Avenue, Roosevelt Road,
Albany Avenue,
and West 19th Street
William Le Baron Jenney 1981
Oscar F. Dubois 1885
Jens Jensen 1906

Douglas Park was one of three commissioned by the West Parks District at its founding in 1869. William LeBaron Jenney, appointed superintendent, imagined the three parks as a unified ensemble, each with its own distinct character. Douglas Park, named after Illinois Senator Stephen Douglas, was intended as the most rustic. Jenney began by excavating a large central lagoon and by filling the low, inhospitable site with manure and sand so large trees and plantings would grow. A portion of the lagoon, whose northern end is framed by iron and stone bridges, survives from Jenney's original design, but the park remained relatively underdeveloped until Jens Jensen took over in 1905. Jensen, a Danish immigrant, started as a laborer for the West Parks in the 1880s. Unlike most landscape architects of the day, who championed a European-style formalism or pastoralism, Jensen was enchanted by the Midwest's natural features. He became active in the Chicago-based Prairie School, a group of writers, artists, and architects that included Frank Lloyd Wright. After rising through the ranks to become general superintendent for the West Parks, Jensen was able to put his ideas into effect. The southern half of Douglas Park shows his influence, where a bermed meadow of regional plantings segues into a woodland landscape of hawthorn trees.

Douglas Park Fieldhouse 23

Douglas Park
Michaelson & Rognstad
1928

The present fieldhouse was built in 1928, replacing an earlier, Prairie-style refectory and music court that had been built under the superintendency of Jens Jensen in 1907. The architectural firm of Michaelson & Rognstad designed several structures for the West Parks Commission in the late 1920s, including the Humboldt Park Fieldhouse nearly identical to this one. A free variation of the Georgian Revival style, this fieldhouse is divided into three main masses. The flat-roofed central section houses a two-story main hall; two-and-a-half story octagonal stair towers with "candle-snuffer" domes articulate the connection between this central section and the lower one and one-half story gymnasium wings, which project at 45 degree angles under hipped roofs. Exterior walls are of red brick laid in a Flemish bond; the classical ornamentation is chiefly of Bedford limestone and includes columns, pilasters, broken pediments, and cornices. Most notable are the many loggias tying the structure to its site. One of cast concrete, at basement level, provides direct access to the lagoon's man-made beach; another, double-story loggia of Tuscan columns graces the main, north facade, while the southern elevation bears a single-story limestone arcade.

24 Flower Hall Group

Ogden Avenue
1907

The Flower Hall Group is the most important example that survives in Douglas Park of Jensen's ideas concerning the integration of architecture, park furniture, and landscape. His refectory and music court, and a pergola at the 19th Street entrance, are now demolished. This complex, on which he is thought to have collaborated with Prairie School architect Hugh M. G. Garden (1873-1961), consists of three basic components: the Flower Hall itself, a formal garden, and a grouping of benches and lamp standards. The Flower Hall, a covered walkway at the southwest end, possesses a classical feel in its symmetry and architectural forms, but with touches of Prairie style in its horizontality and simplified projecting cornices. A tall central pavilion with a giant archway is flanked by arcades and end pavilions. Made of reinforced concrete, its abstracted forms — cube, arch, column, lintel — create a strong visual presence. A reflecting pool forms the transition from this hard geometry to Jensen's softer formal garden. A perimeter sidewalk, curving around the northeast end of the garden, ties the complex together; it is lined by reinforced concrete benches and light standards in the Prairie style, whose precise rectilinearity visually connects it to the Flower Hall to the southwest.

Garfield Park 25

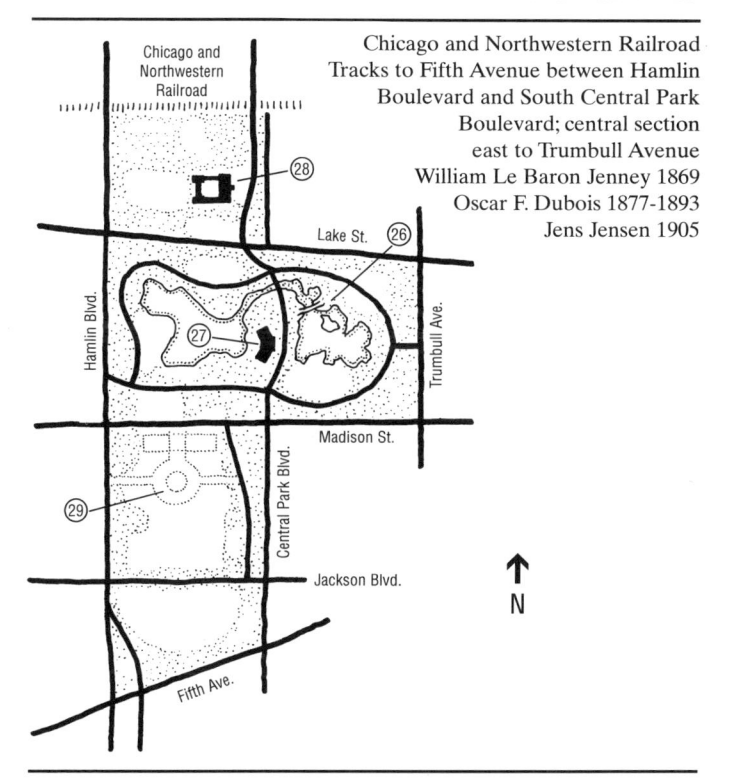

Chicago and Northwestern Railroad Tracks to Fifth Avenue between Hamlin Boulevard and South Central Park Boulevard; central section east to Trumbull Avenue
William Le Baron Jenney 1869
Oscar F. Dubois 1877-1893
Jens Jensen 1905

Garfield (originally Central) Park is the most sophisticated of Jenney's plans for the West Parks system. He aimed to combine the open spaces typical of the grand pleasure grounds of the South Parks with cultural, educational, and athletic facilities. To achieve this goal harmoniously in a mid-size (185-acre) space, Jenney created distinct park precincts delineated by "walls" of trees, and also by city streets. A northern meadow was intended for military parades and team sports (it now hosts the conservatory); the middle portion, provided concert facilities on the west and picnic/play areas on the east, as well as a large lagoon, as in Jenney's other West Parks; the south was reserved for educational facilities such as a natural history museum, never built. Later parks designers significantly altered the plan's design through the 1930s; most notable among them is Jens Jensen, whose regional plantings and Prairie-inspired conservatory are fine examples of his work. Nevertheless, Jenney's original plan is perceptible in the park's rational design, its integration with surrounding streets (including Jenney's planned boulevard system), and the variety of its landscape spaces. Diverse and exuberant architecture also distinguishes this park.

26 Suspension Bridge

Garfield Park
William Le Baron Jenney
1874

Although William LeBaron Jenney designed a comprehensive plan for Garfield Park in 1870, limited funds prevented its development all at once. Jenney recommended starting with the section east of Central Park Boulevard, between Lake and Madison Streets. Opened in 1874, this forty-acre area is considered among the oldest preserved landscaped spaces in Chicago. It also contains one of the few remaining structures built according to Jenney's original plan: this pedestrian suspension bridge, which crosses the eastern lagoon at a narrow point northeast of the fieldhouse. The walkway is composed of wooden planks laid on a span of wooden beams. The span is hung from short iron rods attached to supporting suspension cables, which are anchored, in turn, to concrete pylons at either end of the bridge. An iron handrail with grill borders runs along each side of the walkway. Jenney, trained as an engineer, was a pioneer in the development of the skyscraper as well as a major figure in Chicago's parks design. The engineering skill later displayed in the Second Leiter Building and Manhattan Building (both 1891) is also evident in this small bridge. Stone abutments and piers were replaced with reinforced concrete in 1936, but the original character remains.

District Health Center and Fieldhouse 27

Garfield Park
100 North Central Park Avenue
Michaelson & Rognstad
1928

Formerly West Park Commission Administration Building

The fieldhouse, originally headquarters for the West Parks Commission, is the visual centerpiece of Garfield Park. Located on a peninsula between the east and west lagoons, and on the north-south axis of Central Park Boulevard (which curves here to accommodate it), the building is highly visible in all directions. From the central rectangular mass, two wings with low, hipped roofs extend backward on the northwest and southwest, creating a bow shape. In the central building, a rotunda with a geometric terrazo floor houses four wall panels sculpted by Richard Bock, frequent collaborator with Frank Lloyd Wright. Above it, an enormous octagonal dome, rising 90 feet above grade, is dramatically tiled in gold-leaf terra cotta. The exterior is executed in Spanish Colonial Revival, a style modeled on the Late Baroque cathedrals of Latin America and popularized by the 1915-16 Panama-California Exhibition in San Diego, California. The main entrance, elaborately sculpted of terra cotta, is particularly noteworthy. Twisted Corinthian columns frame three round-arch entrance portals at ground level; upper levels feature arched windows and a statue of LaSalle, the French explorer of the Upper Midwest, vying for attention with an exuberant surround of swags, lion's heads, foliage, and female faces.

28 Garfield Park Conservatory

300 North Central Park Boulevard
Jens Jensen and
Schmidt, Garden & Martin
Hitchings & Co,. engineers
1906-7
Renovation: Chicago Park District 1958

These indoor gardens are a fine example of Jen Jensen's ideas. Unlike Victorian greenhouses with their showy floral displays and potted plants, this conservatory offers integral environments of plantings, stonework, and water that portray the various stages of the Midwestern landscape from prehistoric days to the present. The Fern House, for instance, recreates Illinois' prehistoric conditions: tropical plantings surround a low water cascade whose stratified stonework echoes the banks of Illinois' Rock River (and illustrates one inspiration behind Prairie architecture's horizontality). Five smaller rooms, each with its own climate setting and environment, surround the Fern Room in a rectangle, while the Palm House on the west serves as the entrance. Like the gardens, the structure itself was modeled on native forms. The haystacks Jensen saw across the Midwest in autumn inspired the gently curving form of the Palm House's roof and walls which seem to hug the ground from their concrete base. Though bolder I-beams have replaced the Palm House's lacy trusses, and the translucent panels are now fiberglass, the form remains true to the original design. The Horticulture Hall, by Michaelsen & Rognstad, was added in 1928; a larger vestibule replaced the original in 1958.

Bandstand 29

Garfield Park
Music Court east of Hamlin Avenue
Joseph Lyman Silsbee
1896

William Le Baron Jenney's original 1870 plan for the park called for an "Oriental Terrace" on the western edge of Garfield Park's lagoon, meant to include a bandstand among other amenities. This desire for an Eastern-inspired structure was fulfilled in 1896, though in a different location just south of Madison Street. The architect, Joseph Lyman Silsbee (1848-1913), designed the Garfield Park Power Station in the same year, as well as Lincoln Park's Conservatory (see # 44). He was also known as Frank Lloyd Wright's first employer in Chicago. The bandstand consists of a one-story octagonal podium clad in white Georgia marble, above which an octagonal copper roof is supported on eight octagonal columns. The podium originally contained restrooms, a tool room, and a police station. The open-air platform could accommodate a 100-piece orchestra. Its form and ornament reflect the late-Victorian interest in Islamic styles. A geometric mosaic of blue and green glass tiles encircles the podium. Doorways are set within ogee-arched recesses, also trimmed with mosaics in curvilinear foliate patterns. The copper dome has an underlining of glass mosaics, while bands of curvilinear ornament and a crocket spire decorate its exterior.

30 Columbus Park

West Adams Boulevard, South Central Avenue
Eisenhower Expressway, Austin Boulevard
Jens Jensen
1920

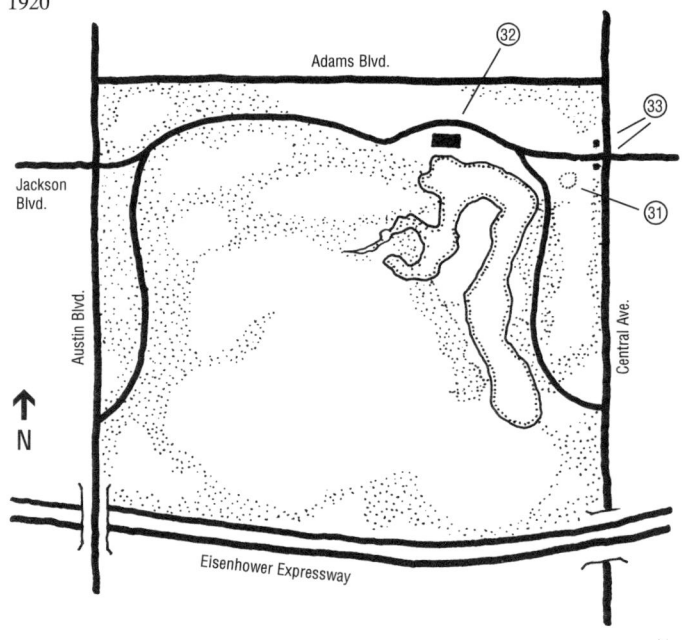

Columbus Park is considered Jen Jensen's masterpiece, his opportunity to design a landscape on one of the last large open tracts annexed to the city of Chicago. The Prairie River is a key component of his design. Originating in twin waterfalls that tumble across stratified rock in the manner of an Illinois river bluff, it then serpentines down the eastern half of the park. Dirt from the excavation was used to build Player's Hill, a place for outdoor performances, as well as for a berm which separates this sylvan interior from recreational facilities on the park's eastern border. To the west, Jensen designed open land whose vista he described evocatively: "looking west from the river bluffs at sundown across a quiet bit of meadow . . . this gives a feeling of breadth and freedom that only the prairie landscape can give to the human soul." A later golf course allows recreational use of this area without disturbing Jensen's desired horizontality. Jackson Boulevard, the main artery to downtown Chicago, could not be excluded from the park but was rerouted to its northern edge. Part of the park was lost in 1955 when the Eisenhower Expressway was built, but recent efforts of the Chicago Park District have restored many of the native plantings.

Council Ring Remnants 31

Jens Jensen
1920

The council ring was a trademark feature of Jens Jensen, who served as superintendent of the West Parks from 1905 to 1920. To Jensen it represented both Native American and Danish folk traditions, wedding elements of his home country with those of the western American landscape he so admired. Usually a low, circular stone set around a fire. The council ring could be used for storytelling, drama, music, or conversation. In Jensen's words: "a ring speaks of strength and friendship and is one of the great symbols of mankind. The fire in the center portrays the beginning of civilization, and it was around the fire our forefathers gathered when they first placed foot on this continent." This council ring, located at the eastern edge of Columbus Park, was intended specifically for storytelling. It is part of the children's playground area, an original segment of Jensen's design that contains an area for free play, a children's shelter, and a wading pool. While many of Jensen's rings were solid benches of stratified stones, here the signature stratified stones form piers, placed at intervals around the circle and topped by a continuous stone seat. The seat has since come unlodged, but the remains convey Jensen's intended effect.

32 Columbus Park Refectory and Boat Landing

Chatten & Hammond
1922
Renovation: Chicago Park District 1992

Jens Jensen desired Columbus Park's buildings to reflect the Prairie style of his landscape design, but the West Parks Commissioners favored more traditional architecture. Growing disagreements, including one over this refectory, eventually led to Jensen's resignation as West Parks superintendent. Though not in Jensen's favored Prairie idiom, the building is nonetheless an attractive Mediterranean Revival structure which takes full advantage of its riverside site. It was designed by Chatten & Hammond in an L-shape plan, consisting of a long rectangular main building and a shorter, perpendicular loggia on the west. Both sections are built of brick with stone trim and have low-pitched hipped roofs of Spanish tile with overhanging eaves. The main building's north and south facades feature six rounded-arch bays separated by fluted Doric pilasters; paned windows fill each bay, flooding the large interior hall with light and offering expansive water views across the terrace. The loggia consists of similar bays and pilasters but is open to the air. Opposite, on the east, a one-story boat dock topped with a balustraded terrace extends into the lagoon. Its rhythmic lines and orientation toward the water make it a pleasing counterpoint to Jensen's treasured prairie river.

Columbus Park Lanterns   33

Jackson Boulevard at Central Avenue
Schmidt, Garden & Martin
1918

These twin lanterns flank the Jackson Boulevard entrance to Columbus Park, leading into the children's playground area with its council ring. On each, a low-pitched hipped copper roof with wide overhanging leaves caps a cast-iron luminaire screen that stands in turn atop a tall, square concrete base. They are classic examples of the Prairie style, an esthetic characterized by clean forms and horizontal lines that was inspired by the regional landscape and made famous by the work of Frank Lloyd Wright. Park designer Jens Jensen was an ardent exponent of the style, as the prairie vistas of this park indicate; so too was the designer of the lanterns, Hugh M. G. Garden, who collaborated frequently with Jensen on buildings and objects in the West Side parks. Indeed, these lanterns are identical to those Garden designed in the same year for the Boat House, Music Court, and Rose Garden areas of Humboldt Park (see # 40). Born in Toronto, Garden began his career as a draftsman in various Chicago offices and as a freelance renderer for Frank Lloyd Wright. He later collaborated with architect Richard E. Schmidt (1865-1958) on many noteworthy Chicago buildings.

34 Humboldt Park

West North Avenue, North Kedzie Avenue, West Augusta Boulevard, North Sacramento Boulevard, West Division Street, North California Avenue Addition: 1912 West Augusta Boulevard, North Whipple Street, West Walton Street, west of North Sacramento Boulevard
William Le Baron Jenney 1871-77
Oscar F. Dubuis 1877-1890s
Jens Jensen 1906-9

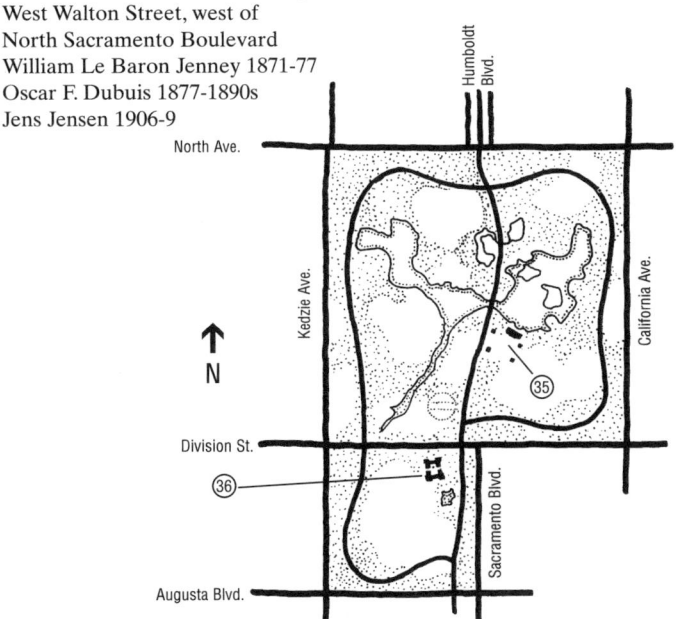

Humboldt Park, named for 19th century German naturalist Alexander von Humboldt, was sited in 1869 amid a German-Polish community on Chicago's expanding northwest border. As in Douglas and Garfield Parks, William Le Baron Jenney originally planned a large lagoon surrounded by pastoral landscapes and winding paths. This design survives in the park's eastern half, where the irregular banks and small islands of the lagoon exemplify Jenney's picturesque ideal. But here as elsewhere Jenney's design was only partially implemented, and coexists with the indigenous landscape aesthetic of his successor, Jens Jensen. Jensen's style is particularly evident in the western half of the park, where he filled much of the lagoon to create a narrower "prairie river" bordered by three large meadows. For the eastern half of the park, Jensen commissioned lanterns, and a boathouse and pavilion from prominent Prairie School architect Hugh M.G. Garden (see # 24 and # 35). Both the prairie river and the lanterns would later reappear in Jensen's masterpiece, Columbus Park (see # 30). Less characteristic of Jensen's work is a bermed, formal rose garden to the east of the river.

Pavilion and Boathouse 35

East side of Humboldt Drive north of Division Street
Richard E. Schmidt, Garden & Martin
1907

To encourage more active enjoyment of the lagoon, park superintendent Jens Jensen commissioned this boathouse and refectory from the firm of architect Hugh M. G. Garden, a frequent collaborator. The long, low structure lies between the eastern lagoon and the Music Court, originally a paved plaza for music concerts and now a parking lot. The boathouse, a one-story, brick structure, occupies the lower level. Due to a change in grade, it is not visible from the Music Court, but on the north side are still visible the six rectangular doorways, now covered over, which once opened directly into the lagoon. The refectory, on the upper level, consists of a central open-air shelter flanked by enclosed rooms, all contained under a low-pitched hipped roof. A row of windows in each flanking room echoes the boathouse doorways below. But the building's focal point is the open-air shelter, defined by three magnificent semicircular arches which provide views of both lagoon and Music Court. The simple and dramatic composition juxtaposes the horizontal sweep of roof and boathouse with the rhythmic curves of the arches, beautifully reflected in the water below.

36 Receptory Building

Frommann and Jebsen
1895-6

When Humboldt Park first opened in 1877 only the eastern 80 acres had been improved; much of the remaining park simply was planned as a temporary nursery. It was not until the 1890s that work began on the southwest section of the park with the construction of a new Receptory Building. This structure served as a receiving place for the park and included stables, storage areas, workshops, and offices. Configured around an open courtyard to facilitate accessibility for horses and wagons, this red-brick half-timbered building was designed in the style of a German countryhouse, with numerous steeply pitched roofs, leaded glass windows (since removed) dormers, turrets and cupolas. Use of this picturesque style shows the influence of German area residents, who had earlier petitioned for the park to be named for German naturalist Frederick Wilhelm Karl Heinrich Alexander von Humboldt (1769-1859). Also noteworthy is the landscape surrounding the Receptory where Jens Jensen, then Superintendent of Humboldt Park, planned a small pond with aquatic plants. Recently restored, the Receptory has been designated as a new Hispanic Cultural Arts Museum, once again reflecting how Chicago's parks respond to and reflect changing neighborhood character and needs.

Lincoln Park 37

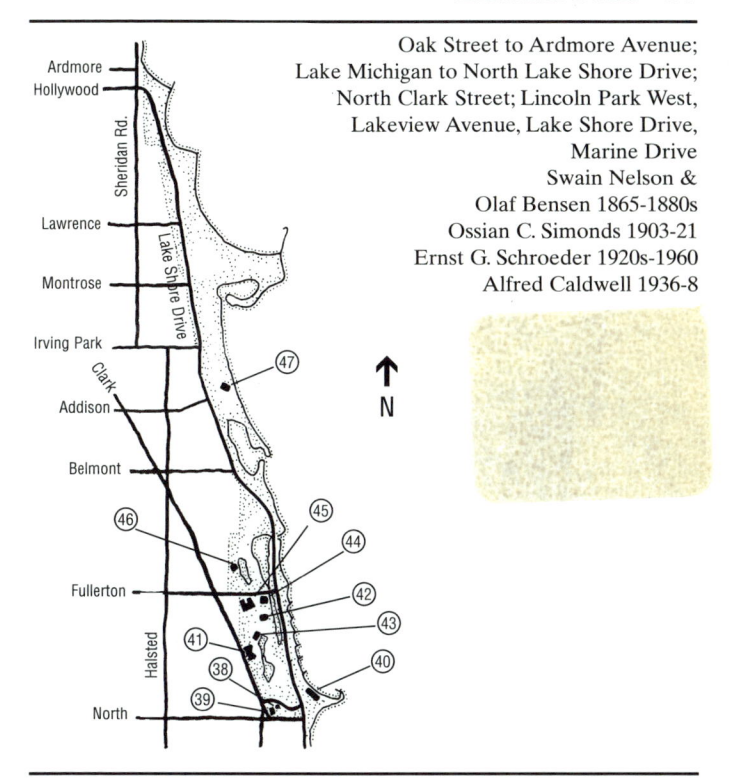

Oak Street to Ardmore Avenue;
Lake Michigan to North Lake Shore Drive;
North Clark Street; Lincoln Park West,
Lakeview Avenue, Lake Shore Drive,
Marine Drive
Swain Nelson &
Olaf Bensen 1865-1880s
Ossian C. Simonds 1903-21
Ernst G. Schroeder 1920s-1960
Alfred Caldwell 1936-8

Established in 1864 and continuously developed for a century, Lincoln Park embodies many ideas of park development in Chicago. Its earliest segments were initially a municipal cemetery. In its second phase, the park was expanded along the lakefront from North Avenue to Diversey Parkway. This segment, designed by Swain Nelson and Olaf Bensen in the mode of 18th-century French gardens, featured small lawns and ponds surrounded by winding paths. The area north to Cornelia Street was filled and developed between 1903 and 1921 under landscape architect Ossian C. Simonds; on this acreage, which includes Belmont Harbor, Simonds employed a more indigenous vocabulary of Midwestern plantings. Engineer Ernst Schroeder, active from the 1920s to the 1960s, oversaw the park's final extension north to Ardmore Avenue, and continued to promote native materials. Most notable from his tenure are landscape architect Alfred Caldwell's Prairie-style Zoo Rookery and Montrose Point. Athletic facilities such as a golf course and tennis courts multiplied in this latest phase, representing a modern concept of the park's social purpose. Offering over seven miles of open lakefront and beaches with museums and monuments set among its plantings, Lincoln Park is the largest and most intensively used park in the Chicago system.

38 Couch Tomb

Between Lake Shore Drive and Clark Street,
just south of the LaSalle Street Connector
Unknown
1858

Ira Couch, an upstate New York native who moved to Chicago in 1837, made a fortune in real estate investment in the burgeoning Loop. His greatest success involved buying the rooming house where he lived and transforming it into Chicago's first luxury hotel. Despite all expectations, Tremont House, popularly called "Couch's folly," became a huge success, and Ira died a millionaire in 1857. In 1858, the family commissioned a mausoleum in the municipal cemetery. Designed to be the city's grandest, the 16' by 10' by 13' structure was built of 100 tons of imported stone and was originally surrounded by gardens and a wrought-iron fence. In 1866, however, the cemetery was deemed a public nuisance, and the land, running from North Avenue to Webster Avenue, became part of newly-founded Lincoln Park. Though the other graves were relocated, the Couch Tomb remained. The reasons for its retention in the park are unknown: family influence, or the prohibitive cost of moving such a heavy structure, may have contributed. Though in disrepair, the tomb still stands on its original plot south of LaSalle Drive, a visible reminder of the pre-Civil War history of this oldest section of Lincoln Park.

Chicago Historical Society 39

Clark Street at North Avenue
Graham, Anderson, Probst and White
1932

Addition: Holabird & Root, 1988

Correction:
Map #47 = Entry #46
Map #46 = Entry #45
Map #45 = Entry #44
Omit Map #44

After World War I, the Chicago Historical Society had outgrown its facilities, still standing, at 632 North Dearborn Street, and a new, larger facility was planned. In 1932, Graham, Anderson Probst and White, a prolific architectural firm (see # 5, and # 6) designed this structure in a Georgian Revival style. Located in the busy southwest corner of Lincoln Park, it is a three-story structure of largely horizontal proportions. The original parkside entrance features a Bedford limestone portico of Roman Doric columns supporting a simple triangular pediment. Bedford limestone was also used for window surrounds, pilasters on the projecting end pavilions, and a rooftop balustrade, while the body of the building is red brick. A 1988 Holabird & Root addition, replacing a 1972 addition by Shaw & Associates, is more consistent with the original building's style. Here a limestone-clad first floor is topped by two stories of red brick; trim is of limestone and white-painted metal. The new main entrance, defined by a recessed three-story metal grid capped by a metal "pediment", reinterprets the original entrance in modern materials. Linked to the main building via a connector glazed in mirrored glass, the addition's rounded southern end provides dramatic view down Clark Street.

40 North Avenue Beach House

Lakefront and North Avenue
E.V. Buchsbaum
1939

Many Chicago parks projects were funded by the Works Progress Administration (WPA) during the Depression, including the improvement of this section of lakefront. Between 1937 and 1941, the paved-edge shore between North Ave. and Fullerton Parkway was converted into a beach, protected by a hood-shaped breakwater. As part of the project, this beach house was commissioned at the beach's southern end, east of the LaSalle Drive interchange with North Lake Shore Drive. It was designed by the Chicago Park District's in-house architect, Emanuel Buchsbaum, who built many structures in Lincoln Park, including utilitarian service buildings and several English Cottage-style comfort stations. Here, however, Buchsbaum responded to the lakefront site with a more whimsical design that reflects the 1930s interest in "modernistic" architecture. Built atop a concrete slab, the one-story, wood-frame structure is clad in flush wood boards, and consists of two wings containing men's and women's bathhouses, connected by a central loggia and covered by a flat roof. The exterior, however, is detailed in a nautical style reminiscent of a lake steamer ship, complete with porthole windows, "smokestacks," and "sail towers," adding to the tradition of fanciful yet functional park architecture.

Chicago Academy of Sciences Building 41

2001 North Clark Street
Patton & Fisher
1893

The cool elegance of the Chicago Academy of Sciences building owes a debt to 18th-century English Neo-Classicism and, ultimately, to Renaissance architect Andrea Palladio. Located just west of Lincoln Park Zoo, its visual focus is the main entrance facing Clark Street, which consists of three round arches approached via a broad staircase. Above, limestone columns with terra cotta Corinthian capitals support a triangular terra cotta pediment, ornamented with the building's date, 1893. On the upper walls, terra cotta moldings surround blind recessed arches, originally windows that were filled soon after construction. The hipped roof and central transverse gable are clad with clay tile. The building was designed for the Chicago Academy of Sciences, an institution founded in 1857 to promote knowledge of the region's natural history. The complementary interests of the Academy and the Lincoln Park Zoo led to the offer of this site, and construction funds were supplied by prominent pioneer Matthew Laflin, whose memorial stands just above the entrance. Vacated by the Academy in 1995 as part of a property swap between the Chicago Park District and the Lincoln Park Zoological Society, the building was recently renovated as the Zoological Society's new headquarters.

42 Lincoln Park Zoo Lion House

Lincoln Park Zoo
Perkins, Fellow & Hamilton
1912

The Lincoln Park Zoo was established in 1868 when New York City's Central Park donated two pairs of swans to Chicago. The earliest zoo structures were little more than decorative cages, but by the early 20th century, a need was felt for larger, permanent structures containing more naturalistic habitats. The Lion House, one of the oldest permanent structures in the Lincoln Park Zoo, is also one of the most architecturally significant. It consists of a central exhibit hall flanked by outdoor viewing areas: a large open space with artificial rocks on the north, and a series of outdoor cages on the south. The exhibit hall, constructed in reddish-brown brick with terra cotta trim, is noted for its beautiful detailing. On the east and west facades, large arched entrances are flanked by pairs of lion silhouettes, while the upper areas are ornamented with tile set in a grid pattern. Inside, a vaulted and ribbed tile ceiling is pierced with clerestory windows. Perkins, Fellows & Hamilton was formed in 1911 as the successor firm to Perkins & Hamilton who designed Cafe Brauer (see # 43); for this design, the firm won a Gold Medal from the Illinois chapter of the American Institute of Architects in 1912.

Café Brauer 43

2021 North Stockton Drive
Perkins & Hamilton
1908
Renovation: Lawrence B. Berkley & Associates;
Meisel & Associates; Wiss, Janney, Elstner Associates 1989

Built by Perkins & Hamilton in 1908, Café Brauer exemplifies Prairie-style architecture adapted for park use. Dwight Perkins, a close friend to noted Prairie landscaper Jens Jensen, was a nationally-known designer of schools; here, he and engineer J. L. Hamilton designed a symmetrical building dominated by a central, two-story pavilion. Smaller end pavilions, also two stories high, are connected to it via brick arcades supporting open-air dining terraces. The entire composition curves slightly, nestling into the adjacent South pond. The walls are made of variegated red, green, and brown brick laid with red mortar, and ornamented with green terra cotta tiles. This emphasis on building materials' inherent color and texture reflects the continued influence of Arts and Crafts ideals in the work of progressive Chicago architects such as Perkins. The horizontality associated with Prairie School buildings is emphasized by raking the horizontal mortal joints and leaving the vertical joints flush; overhanging eaves on the clay-tile hipped roof enhance the Prairie effect. Paul and Caspar Brauer, who financed the building, ran a successful restaurant here until 1941; an excellent restoration, including interior spaces like the soaring, skylight-capped Great Hall, was finished in 1989.

44 Lincoln Park Conservatory

Stockton Drive between Belden and Fullerton Parkway
Joseph Lyman Silsbee
1894

Architect Joseph L. Silsbee made his name in Chicago with house designs, including the Romanesque-influenced Horatio May House on North Astor Street and several Queen Anne row houses at Clark Street and Dickens Avenue. For the Lincoln Park commissioners he designed this conservatory in the tradition of 19th century greenhouses, with large glass-and-iron enclosures to provide micro-climates for tropical plants. Mifflin Bell designed the propagating houses to the rear. Built on a granite base, the building's framework consists of copper glazing bars holding individual panes of both clear and translucent wire glass. The tiered roofs are profiled in a bell-cast, hipped configuration. The main entry was remodeled in the 1950s to accommodate public restrooms and is clad in stone. Located in the earliest-developed part of Lincoln Park, just south of Fullerton Parkway, the building is surrounded by other 19th century designs. The 1887 Bates Fountain (Storks at Play) stands in a formal French-style garden to the south; to the west, across Stockton Drive, is the informal, English-style Grandmother's Garden and an 1894 statue of Shakespeare by W. O. Partridge.

Rustic Pavilion   45

Lakeview Avenue at St. James Place
Mifflin E. Bell
1883

Built in 1883, the Rustic Pavilion is one of the oldest structures in Lincoln Park. Located east of Stockton Drive, on an axis with St. James Place, it stands on the western bank of North Pond and originally covered an artesian well. A second rustic shelter, also covering an artesian well, stood on the east bank of the pond, opposite the existing structure; it is now demolished. Architect Mifflin E. Bell worked with Joseph Lyman Silsbee on the nearby Lincoln Park Conservatory, and like Silsbee, he designed handsome residences, including the Queen Anne-style Theodore Rice house in Hyde Park (1892). In contrast to those structures, here he designed this open-air pavilion in a deliberately "primitive" style. Rough-hewn wooden posts support an octagonal roof composed of wooden rafters, tongue-and-groove decking, and sheet metal. After a 1990 paint analysis, the pavilion was repainted with its original colors: the roof is beige, while wooden posts and cross braces are light brown. Inside the shelter, a sky-blue ceiling stands against exposed beams highlighted in yellow.

46 Waveland Field House and Brett's Cafe (Refectory)

East of Lake Shore Drive opposite Waveland Avenue
Edwin H. Clark
1932

The Waveland Field House and Carillon Tower was constructed as one component of the expansion of Lincoln Park northward in the 1910s and 1920s. New landfill between Cornelia and Montrose Avenues was designated as a golf course in 1928, and architect Edwin Clark was commissioned to build an adjacent restaurant and golf shelter. As tennis courts and athletic fields were added to the plan, the shelter was upgraded to a fieldhouse. Collegiate Gothic in style, the building is oriented on a north-south axis and has short, transverse wings on each end. Walls are red brick with Bedford limestone trim, while the gabled roofs are clad with variegated purple and green slate. Loggias facing east and west access interior locker rooms which have terrazzo floors and walls clad in unglazed tan brick. Clark, who also designed the Aquarium and Primate House in the Lincoln Park Zoo, altered his design to accommodate a last-minute commission. Anna Wolford, who had nostalgic memories of chimes from Massachusetts vacations, provided funds for a tower with carillon and clock; Clark placed the four-story tower asymmetrically, toward the north end of the building. Volunteers repaired the clock and chimes, both long inoperative, in 1992.

Glossary

Acroteria: A pedestal at the corners and peak of a roof to support a statue or ornament; more usually, the ornament itself.

Antefix(ae): A decorated upright slab used in classical architecture to close or conceal the open end of a row of tiles which cover the joints of roof tiles.

Arcade: A series of arches supported by columns or piers; a building or part of a building with a series of arches.

Architrave: The ornamental moldings around the faces of the jambs and lintel of a doorway or window.

Bas-Reliefs: A carving, embossing, or casting moderately protruding from the background plane, derived from the French, meaning "low relief".

Belvedere: A roof-top pavilion from which a vista can be enjoyed.

Cantilever: A projecting beam or part of a structure supported only at one end.

Cartouche: An ornamental panel in the form of a scroll, circle or oval, often bearing an inscription.

Cast Iron: Smelted iron shaped in a mold whose compressive or lead-bearing strength made it an important structural metal.

Chicago School of Architecture: Highrise commercial buildings designed in Chicago in the late 19th century made possible by elevators and linked by constructional similarities, including the use of a metal structural frame to support the building; bay, oriel or Chicago windows to admit maximum light; and the use of the latest wind-bracing and foundation technologies.

Chicago Window: A window occupying the full width of the bay and divided into a large fixed sash flanked by a narrow movable sash at each side.

Glossary

Coffering: a ceiling with deeply recessed, often highly ornamented panels.

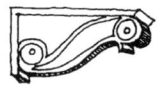

Console: A decorated bracket in the form of a vertical scroll, projecting from a wall to support a cornice, door, or window head.

Cornice: A projecting ornamental molding along the top of a building, wall, arch, etc., finishing or crowning it.

Crocket: In Gothic architecture, an upward-oriented ornament, often vegetal in form, regularly spaced along sloping or vertical edges of spires, pinnacles or gables.

Esplanade: A level open space for walking or driving, often providing a view.

Flying Buttress: A characteristic feature of gothic construction in which the lateral thrust of a roof or vault is taken up by a bar of masonry, usually sloping, carried on an arch, and a solid pier sufficient to receive the thrust.

Light Well: An open area in the center of buildings used to provide natural light and ventilation, prior to the widespread use of electricity and air conditioning, for the rooms or offices contained in the surrounding sides of the building.

Mullion: A vertical member separating and often supporting windows, doors, or panels set in a series.

Ogee: a double curved, formed by the union of a convex and concave line resembling an S-shape.

Pediment: In classical architecture, the triangular gable end of a roof above the horizontal cornice; more commonly, the triangular or curved ornament used over doors or windows.

Glossary

Piano Nobile: In Renaissance architecture, a floor with formal reception rooms, usually one floor above the ground.

Plan of Chicago (1906-09): The City of Chicago's first comprehensive planning document, which included developing efficient transportation systems and waterfront beautification projects. It was informed by Beaux Arts principles of grand boulevards, monuments, and other civic improvements.

Prairie School of Architecture: A midwestern movement that sought to create buildings, chiefly residential, that reflected the flat, horizontal midwestern terrain and used distinctive stylized floral or geometric patterns.

Quatrefoil: A four-lobed pattern divided by cusps.

Rustication: Masonry cut in massive blocks separated from each other by deep joints.

Setback: An architectural epedient in which the upper stories of a tall building are stepped back from the lower stories; designed to permit more light to reach street level.

Skeleton Frame: A free-standing frame of iron or steel that supports the weight of a building and on which the floors and outer covering are hung.

Soffit: The underside of any architectural element.

Spandrel: In a multistory building, a wall panel filling the space between the top of a window in one story and the sill of the window in the story above.

Tempietto: A small temple, esp. one of an ornamental character, during Renaissance or later.

Terra Cotta: Cast and fired clay bricks, usually more intricately modeled than bricks, and used for decorative and/or fireproofing purposes.

Trunnion Bascule Bridge: A type of span that moves in a vertical plane about a horizontal axis and is supported by an axle or trunnion pin, about which it rotates.

Acknowledgements

We would like to thank Howard Decker and Joan Pomaranc for their help and support on this project.

Victoria Behm, graphic designer, writer and illustrator of books on travel, mythology and architecture.

Nicole Ferentz and Brian Doyle, cover design and book production.

Samantha Lee Kelly, editor and historian.

Judith Paine McBrien, President of Perspectives International Inc., writer and film producer of books and programs on architecture, history and design.

Debra McQueen, (buildings) **and Malcolm Edgerton** (maps and details), Debra McQueen Architects, designers and illustrators.

Raymond Tatum, researcher and historian.